A FRAGILE CITY

Micheal O'Siadhail was born in 1947. He was educated at Clongowes Wood College, Trinity College Dublin, and the University of Oslo. A full-time writer, he has published nine collections of poetry. In 1982 he was awarded an Irish American Cultural Institute prize for poetry. His poem suites, *The Naked Flame* and *Summerfest*, were commissioned and set to music for performance and broadcasting.

Hail! Madam Jazz: New and Selected Poems (Bloodaxe Books, 1992) includes selections from six of his collections, *The Leap Year* (1978), *Rungs of Time* (1980), *Belonging* (1982), *Springnight* (1983), *The Image Wheel* (1985), as well as the whole of *The Chosen Garden* (1990) and a new collection *The Middle Voice* (1992). His latest collection is *A Fragile City* (Bloodaxe Books, 1995).

He has given poetry readings and broadcast extensively in Ireland, Britain and North America. In 1985 he was invited to give the Vernam Hull lecture at Harvard and the Trumbull Lecture at Yale University. He represented Ireland at the Poetry Society's European Poetry festival in London in 1981. He was writer-in-residence at the Yeats Summer School in 1991.

He has been a lecturer at Trinity College Dublin and a professor at the Dublin Institute for Advanced Studies. Among his many academic works are *Learning Irish* (Yale University Press, 1988) and *Modern Irish* (Cambridge University Press, 1989). He was a member of the Arts Council of the Republic of Ireland (1988-93) and is a member of the Advisory Committee on Cultural Relations, a member of Aosdána (Academy of distinguished Irish artists) and a former editor of *Poetry Ireland Review*. He is a board member of The Dublin International Writers' Festival and chairman of ILE (Ireland Literature Exchange).

A FRAGILE CITY

MICHEAL O'SIADHAIL

BLOODAXE BOOKS

ISBN: 1 85224 334 1

First published 1995 by
Bloodaxe Books Ltd,
P.O. Box 1SN,
Newcastle upon Tyne NE99 1SN.

Bloodaxe Books Ltd acknowledges
the financial assistance of Northern Arts.

Cover printing by J. Thomson Colour Printers Ltd, Glasgow.

Printed in Great Britain by
Cromwell Press Ltd, Broughton Gifford, Melksham, Wiltshire.

For Brendan Kennelly

Acknowledgements

Acknowledgements are due to the editors of the following publications in which some of these poems first appeared: *Chapman, Christmas in Ireland* (Mercier Press, 1985), *Gown, Irish Times, Krino, London Magazine, Orbis, Oxford Poetry, Poetry Book Society Anthology 2* (PBS/Hutchinson, 1991), *Poetry Durham, Poetry Ireland Review, Rhinoceros, Stand* and *Stet*; and to RTE Radio and WBEZ, Chicago where a number of the poems were broadcast.

The first three epigraphs are from the following editions: *Selected Poems of Rainer Maria Rilke*, translated by Robert Bly (Harper & Row, 1981); *Selected Writings* by Mirjam Tuominen, translated by David McDuff (Bloodaxe Books, 1994); and *Complete Poems* by Karin Boye, translated by David McDuff (Bloodaxe Books, 1994).

Contents

ʽΟ χόσμος οὗτος μία πόλις ἐστί.
This world of ours is one city.

EPICTETUS

FILTERED LIGHT

Euch kommt jeden Morgen das neue Licht
warm in die offene Wohnung.
Und ihr habt ein Gefühl von Gesicht zu Gesicht,
und das verleitet zur Schonung.

Every morning new light comes
warmly into the open house
and you have a feeling that moves from face to face
and that leads you astray to caring.

RAINER MARIA RILKE
translated by Robert Bly

Transit

Urgencies of language: check-in, stand-by, take-off.
Everything apace, businesslike. But I'm happy here
Gazing at all the meetings and farewells. I love
To see those strangers' faces quickened and bare.
A lost arrival is wandering. A moment on edge,
He pans a lounge for his countersign of welcome.
A flash of greeting, sudden lightening of baggage,
As though he journeyed out only to journey home.
I watch a parting couple in their embrace and freeing.
The woman turns, a Veronica with her handkerchief
Absorbing into herself a last stain of a countenance.
She dissolves in crowds. An aura of her leaving glance
Travels through the yearning air. Tell me we live
For those faces wiped into the folds of our being.

Folding

Our summer hide-out was the crotch of an old sumac,
A bole V-ing upwards into its light and pliancy,
Our feet in the fork, its boughs against our back;
A huddle of inclusiveness, first inkling of diversity.
Who was that strange child, that face at the rim
Demanding vision? It's as if our tree contracted,
Refusing the danger of renewal. A closing system.
That face returns and returns where never expected:
The Jewish woman in Chicago whose stare was rife
With memory or that Aran widower unfurling his story.
We seem to fold into each other, upsurges of a life
Drawing me into a seamless time, their past
A vibrancy of absence leaving its traces in me.
Is the child at the rim every stranger I've faced?

Beyond

Ask me then and I'm almost sure I'd say
A hand, a turn of shoulder, some voluptuous
Bend of playfulness kept inviting my caress.
Those days I talked of *truth* and *beauty*.
It was your expression. Those eyes that welcomed
Without reserve. Open-faced, so much a brother's
Keeper. It's as though we surrendered each other's
Freedom, freeing the other the more we succumbed.
It was years later I thought of Dante's Beatrice,
And how once you'd chided me for making fun
Of an old man. *Who knows what he's undergone?*
A face is filtering light from beyond a face.
You'd seen transparence in a stranger's infinite
Gaze. I moved in your light to see the light.

News

It was a struggle, but he arrived just after one.
Daniel George his father names him by telephone.
An unbroken line. And so he enters our universe
God's my judge, Soil-worker as his grandfathers.
Who's he like? I try to imagine his countenance
A little smudged, but finding its own structure
From genes and traces, incessant recommencements
Travelling towards a future. A recourse and rupture.
It's as though two separatenesses had come together
Blending their need with desire, a self and other,
Some kind of surplus in a lovers' touch and go.
Daniel George. One face of renewal and overflow.
Yours and not yours. You are and are not your son.
Fecundity's old riddle and a world moving on.

Quartet

These players nod and gleam as if they're seeing
And hearing the other's expression, each leaning
Into the fine-nerved strings, their whole being
Vested in this interplay, this gamble on meaning.
I remember a crescendo dream. We burned and burned.
Maybe it's age. I grow in this mutual succumbing:
Bow and pluck, phrase and breath of an earned
And watchful passion, our face to face becoming.
All shall be equal we'd said. But nothing matches.
Overlaps. Voice-overs. A sudden fertile digression
Loops into our rousing silence. Something over-reaches
Equality, a lived-in music shaping my compassion.
The conversation dips and wanders and tenses again.
A shining between faces, a listening inward and open.

Flare

There we were a cluster of twenty-year-olds.
A colour, a timbre fixes the sweep of that mood:
Cheap Chianti, candlelight, damp sugar-bowls,
A readiness to change a world half-understood.
No, nothing could ever again be the same.
Raise a mug of wine, a hymn to the proletariat.
The system's so damned unfair. But we had a dream.
We shall overcome. We'll sing our hearts out.
That chorus and I recall how our faces would blur
Into sameness. *Deep in my heart I still believe.*
Was it a cry for meaning we'd begun to squander,
Our well-meant vision turned faceless and assertive?
An energy flickers the untrimmed wick of a dream.
Our innocent anger keeps scattering the flame.

Focus

Our hurried need to flare and blaze both ends.
How slowly we'd grow, option by tiny option.
Catch us again, now that a fifth decade bends
Our lived-in dream, a jet of steadied vision.
Maybe I've learned to fear the sweeping chorus:
The masses, the system. Something cuts deeper.
Remember how young compassion first moved us:
A solo beseeching face calling me its keeper?
I reach across those years to re-focus a dream
Throwing its light again as our chorus fades;
My cupped hands sheltering the glow of a flame,
I see now in those eyes where their story leads.
Each life is thickening into its own fabric.
Every face so utterly itself. Alone. Unique.

Tension

The wrong voice, self-righteous, somehow out of tune:
Mr Chairman, I object to my colleague's actions.
One by one around the table we cast our stone.
He put a good face on it. Then, I saw he winced.
But where have I seen those hunted eyes before?
Frenchie, let's get Frenchie! The victim's glance
As he bolted hell for leather up a school corridor;
The patent shoes and corduroys, a swarthy difference.
I know the rules, but I want to halt this sacrifice.
My neighbour whispers: 'he's got to be taken to task,
A question of solidarity'. Does a fish squirm in a net?
I'm full of qualms. Was it just the tone of voice?
A face forgets a face breathing behind a mask.
The heart and the mind. Tensing poles of a magnet.

Casualty

She's at it again. Of course, she'll never learn.
Once she touches the stuff – well, that's that.
I read about it and know this classic pattern:
No insight and rock-bottom always too late.
We go on and on talking. All those far-fetched
Excuses, this ravelling of schemes and make-believe.
Am I the theory-man, trying to keep us detached?
History judges history and here's a write-off.
But her mother and sister are up again tonight.
The pancreas. Someone must drive her to casualty.
And besides there's the child; such a fright
Could bring his asthma on. In their fuss and care
I turn towards a countenance so alone and singular.
Something in her tragedy faces and outfaces me.

Revelation

Our train gains ground into the evening light.
Among the trees the sun catches in its fall
Glints and anglings of a stone in a distant gable,
A broadcast of facets, one and infinite.
I glance at you. There's so much unexplained.
Plays of your light keep provoking my infinity;
Already something in your presence overflows me,
A gleam of a face refusing to be contained.
How little I know of you. Again and again
I've resolved to be the giver and not the taker,
Somehow to surpass myself. Am I the mapmaker
So soon astray in this unknowable terrain?
Twenty-one years. And I'm journeying to discover
Only what your face reveals. Stranger and lover.

Translation

The tiler was deaf and dumb. He charmed all
With blue-eyed nods and signs until we forgot
His blemish. He pencilled needs on a bare wall:
2 ornamentals, 7 borders, $^1/_2$ tub of grout.
One morning, his thumb and index shape a ring,
As he motions me aside to show a snapshot.
His face glows in this lover's mute naming
But a forefinger signals 'I'm slitting my throat'.
I smile at shyness, a sudden boyish withdrawal.
Is freedom our knowing that freedom is at stake?
He's young and hot in his leather. So I translate
Across trusting years into our male tick-tack.
My palms curve in the air a female figure 8.
I blow from my fingertips a kiss of approval.

Light

She tires easily, I'm warned, just a short while.
Well past ninety, a voyage fulfilled and intense.
I bend to kiss her. She smiles her girl's smile,
A presence begun absenting itself from a presence.
Surely she must be aware she's about to depart.
A strange translucence, an expression almost younger
And keener, as if she's taking the world to heart.
A boundless desire, a hunger nourished by hunger.
She has heard on the news of a newly discovered star,
A billion years it must journey our empty spaces;
The immensity of a conversation's flow and counterflow
Commands me with eyes I seem to answer to and for.
Beauty is truth, truth beauty. That is all ye know...
What is this light that falls between two faces?

Aversion

In fair Verona where we lay our scene. The theatre's
Warm as a festering London. Juliet and her banished
Romeo dally in the orchard, menders of their begetters'
Grudges. *Some shall be pardon'd and some punished.*
Another plot vibrates in me. A Norwegian ('The Slut'
She's called) flees with a German soldier, chooses
Her sweet, neutral days cooped in a Swedish hut.
They're found and shot. *A plague on both your houses.*
Cleansed and resolved, I exit headily to the street.
Of all people, look who's approaching! – a colleague
Who'd always done me down. I want our gaze to meet,
A single gesture. Enough dissembling and intrigue.
A glance averted and we've passed each other by.
Our long fallen history, one twinkling of an eye.

VEILS AND MASKS

Bortom era ord anade jag era ansikten.
De ansikten ni bär är inte era verkeliga.
Ni var förklädda maskerade beslöjade.
Era obeslöjade ansikten är vakrare...

Beyond your words I sensed your faces.
The faces you bear are not your real ones.
You were disguised masked veiled.
Your unveiled faces are more beautiful...

MIRJAM TUOMINEN
translated by David McDuff

Intrusion

The glaze of loved and lover,
our amorous self-containment,
concentric and utterly present
to the other. Sweetest hour.

But what if between our gazes
shadows of the stricken fall,
the stares we seem to veil
keep on commanding us?

Our two-ness is never alone.
Whose is that intrusive face
that looms unseen between us
condemning all we haven't done?

The eclipsed. The destitute.
O sly worm of dominance
coiling its own discountenance,
our masks and blottings out.

Is love a threadbare blindfold?
'Yes,' say our shadows, 'unless
you turn to face the faceless.'
Who'll re-envisge the world?

How?

When the time comes, how will we have been:
giver or hoarder, sharers or sleek *gringos*?
Children of the barrio, how can I explain?

Silk I love: fall and flow and cocoon,
the worm's sheen, desire clinging and loose.
When the time comes, how will we have been?

And fruits: plums, tangerines, seedy moon
of a kiwi, yellow-orange flesh of mangos,
children of the barrio, how can I explain?

Or cheeses skinned with peppers, a stilton
waxy, wrinkle-rinded, my blue-veined gorgonzolas.
When the time comes, how will we have been?

Morning curtains, towels lilac and green
in the light, the pile of a rug scuffing toes,
children of the barrio, how can I explain?

Something cries its grievance. A false coin
is spinning: heads I win, tails you lose.
When the time comes, how will we have been?
Children of the barrio, how can I explain?

Outsider

A sheltered arch or where underground
kitchens of an inn sent
through grids of pavement grating
the warmth of the ass's breath –
Where did last night's Christ lie down?

Every morning for months I watched
a man I might have been,
about my age and bearded too,
his face blotched crimson
with cheap wine and sleeping rough.

He walked the far side of the street
always hurrying somewhere;
a father who couldn't praise, I wondered,
or what had blurred his star?
For months our eyes never met,

though the street between us was narrow,
until that eve he crossed.
'Some help,' he said, but it must have been
my double's eyes that asked
where would He lie down tomorrow?

An old outsider within me winced,
shook him off and fled;
that street between was so narrow –
I chose the inn and was afraid.
I'm sure I've never seen him since –

but tomorrow when carafes go round
a lone presence will pass
tremors through our frail togetherness;
again those eyes will ask
where did last night's Christ lie down?

Tables

1

'You know yourself, nothing but money counts.'
I try my best to smile my knowing smile.
Nods to an age's spirit, a self-effacement.

So often he's the enabler, a hidden hand lent.
'On bread alone?' But any doubt is scandal.
I swallow mutinous words as the tables turn.

What did I ever know of deprivation? His scorn
whips me: shame, insecurity, angst that haunts
a body all its life. Nothing. I know nothing.

Self-made, yet so many taken under his wing.
Even innocence must sometimes wear a mask.
'That's talk for acsetics or the too well-off!'

2

An ascetic? No. A mortal who loves to eat
sharon fruits, blancmange, to sip iced rosé
or feel warm sand on the arches of his feet.

Young Keats dressed and quiffed for his table.
I bath early, grooming and scenting myself;
silked and rakish, I'm ready to love invisible

muses. Then everything cloys except the journey.
Endless desert. I feed on some hump of memory
and expectation. Ecstasy moving and stationary,

a delight fuelling itself. Unlimited supply
and demand. The end of desire is more desire.
My camel soul must travel the needle's eye.

3

He's sleeping rough. There but for a woman's praise
assuaging my temperament. (Who'll shelter my double?)
I tuck my knee-caps into the hollows of her knees.

And still he haunts me, my vagabond counterpart.
I know Thomas More brought beggars to his table.
Every loop of the mind I try keeps falling short.

So much dereliction I know I can't countenance.
Justice is a faceless scales. Tell me who'll be
the rich man sighting that prodigal in the distance

to fall on his neck and kiss him? The love cup
raised in celebration of a father's huge abandon;
the art of giving, the art of never giving up.

Hostel

Station of ease for the broken or frail.
A tear in an ocean. And yet that welcome
At face value, a roof and warmth, a meal.
Vague signals of angeldom.

So little. So short of grand revolution
We'll always want to dream of.
If only dreams could scoop or fill an ocean...
Thimbled gestures of a love,

Some gift of falling for endless tasks
Berth this moment's care;
The scarred visage of a down-and-out who asks
If an ocean starts with a tear?

Patient logs of strays and have-nots.
A youth stubborn and hurt
Uproots and wanders. No one knows his whereabouts,
Nomad and introvert.

Long headstrong years on the loose;
Now shattered and underfed
A quarrelsome body yields nightly to delicious
Mercies of bath and bed.

One evening and again he's gone
Without trace. No mendings. No rebirth.
Tiny alleviations, something beautiful done.
A caress on the face of the earth.

Theft

Another wired photograph of an African woman
Holding a small girl with a pear-shaped head
And a shrivelled crowfooted face. Has someone
Thieved a child, left her this elf instead?

Drought. Failed crops. And the rains too late.
Hollows of famine rumble the bowels of the earth.
Look long and deep. Unable to clean forget,
I begin my day, busy in the lap of the north.

Little knoweth the fat what the lean doth mean.
I can't ghost-write a suffering. Only my guess
And leap, flickers of memory or the unforeseen.
I know how easily a world unsheathes my tinyness.

But nothing appeases her stare. Again I'll pore
Over this image of hunger. Is compassion a guilty
Fear of *there but for fortune* or is there more?
It's as though something in her gaze commands me.

A look both rapt and implacable. There's no wool
To pull over these eyes. Look long. Look deeper.
Cycles of dominance; a hemisphere's rise and fall.
She stares and stares. Am I my sister's keeper?

Two After Dark

1

I tuned in that night to a man's ageing voice:
'I'm fancy-free. I could have had my pick of them.'
An eavesdropper, had I already begun to pity him?

'Maybe if you're tethered young, you get used to it.
All you needed was the gab and a good way with you.
On the dance-floor I was as smart as any on my feet.

'Out there with a steady, if I saw a handsomer woman
I'd watch my chance. *But haven't you a girl with you?
It's you I want,* I'd say, *and sure don't mind anyone.'*

I stare at a wireless trying to envisage his face.
'And I did a great trade in women from far and near.'
An old notched gun smoking stubbornly in the corner.

2

I remembered sitting in half-light with an old friend
Stitching years we'd missed. But as night came on
I knew I'd heard her hearing my unasked question.

'I waited,' she laughed, 'for a prince to come riding
On a white horse.' Always one of us, she'd refused
To flatter or fawn; confidante and equal in everything.

A nature that had to give all. Why anything less?
She used to say 'Wait till I'm minister for fairness!'
Just wait. That was a time when we owned the world.

Men. Where will they all fade with their giddiness?
No prince. She rose, making her way across the dark
To a lamp, luminous and surefooted in her apartness.

Rowing Back

If she broached him near the bone, like his father
He'd abscond, then, reappear in his boat to pout
For hours on end in the bay, sitting it out
Till she came beckoning guiltily from the shore.

I see him there shame-faced, glad of a let-out,
As hunching on his oars he turned and back-tracked,
Sullen but somehow holding his maleness intact,
Frail dignity balanced on the keel of a boat.

Come clean. What is it we've been so afraid of?
A fear of what we couldn't tame, wild otherness
Wobbling and ungraspable, a sway and completeness.
We row an unfathomable sea. Comber and trough.

Tumble and come-back. A filling tide's action
And passivity, slow logic of retreats and charges,
As wave into wave keeps gaining on itself, surges
Beyond our control and so full of direction.

But something in her expression is veiled and denied.
Those old patterns of huff, guilt and climb-down.
The ghosts of so many women are standing alone
Waving to an oarsman brooding on his phantom pride.

Is the boat in the bay cradling a dread of failure,
A bravado trying to face up to its loss of face?
Visible and invisible as children cribbing disgrace
Behind our fingers, forgive us as we row ashore.

At the Hairdresser's

My neck on the porcelain rim, a tautness unbends
Backwards into suds and rushes and squirts of water.
A teenage girl (she could easily be my daughter)
Gentles my head. Surely a world is safe in her hands?
Through the steamy towels and scissorings a radio
Blurts news from the East. Some million men dug in.
Our sly litany, old stealthy dream of domination:
Silkworm, jaguar, tomcat, hawkeye, sea-sparrow.
Her thumbs spiral deep into a skull of memory.
Sully's and Quinner's gangs fight for a school fort
With hedge-cuttings bound into whips. Lash and hurt
And threat of 'sissy' or 'coward'. Above all, don't cry.
My clogged maleness loosens in her determined fingers.
Those helmeted faces so boyish with their unspilt tears.

Embrace

The evening guests arrive, all flowers and wine
and loud hellos at the gate. *Come on, come in.*
Good to see you! Just a bottle for the kitchen.
I kiss the women's cheeks; between us, the men,
a handshake, our gesture and show of strength,
this double signal – hands-on and armslength.

I want to fling my limbs open and embrace.
A clumsy left hand glances a shoulder blade
and I know at once he's feeling some hand laid
to measure a deal's anxiety, nervous give-aways.
A hug is a dagger too close, a dealer's grope.
Something tightens at my touch and buttons up.

I'll take your coat. Flowers. You shouldn't have!
We shy from such receiving, a chink in the male
like a sideways revelation and a hurried withdrawal
or some blurted late-night confidence brushed off
in a morning-after silence or averted look.
Was I bad? I remembered nothing when I woke.

What have we done to ourselves? Years of tautness,
a gaucheness hiding its face behind our ritual,
a coil and wriggle in ourselves we want to veil.
Look! how those women caress and touch with ease.
Sisters, sisters, it's us you're trying to free;
more than your scorn, our dealer's grope needs pity.

And weren't you women once those mothers drying
up our tears? A face shown and withdrawn.
Slugs and snails and puppy dogs. *Stand like a man.*
Tell me, did you ever see your father crying?
A coin's faces, each a keeper for the other.
Woman and man, somehow we're in this together.

Tracks

1

How it sways in its tracks as it gathers speed!
We steady ourselves against any lurch of intimacy,
our deflected faces guarding invisible territory.

The jolted halt, the scurried terrazzo passage,
as elbow to elbow we show our tickets and wedge
towards morning. So much changed and unchanged.

Thousands of years, of mornings, of jostling men:
hunters, tool-users, ranchers, traders, explorers.
Defining. Redefining. Makers and crossers of borders.

Thousands of years, of mornings, of nourishing women,
protectors of inlands, rearers, nurturers, faithful
guardians of hearth, keepers of hive and churn.

We're shoulder to shoulder in this rush and scrum
of a morning. Subtler and more persistent, you wear
our masks and will outwit us. But was there a dream?

The train moves on, grumbling in the frame of a bridge
like a man moaning the linear premise of his station,
a zigzag of life swerving on its narrow gauge.

Our crush on living daylight tapers forwards.
When will you come bringing the milk and honey,
spilling a heartland over our rigid borders?

2

I'd waited all afternoon for her to return.
I glanced through a window at an empty road
of nunnish spruces, tall and dark and stern,
watching over asphalt where it had snowed
on and off, a vague but persistent caress
of muslin laid across a road's aloneness.

Hours delayed, she came laden with apologies:
a colleague ill – someone had to cover for him,
a report due tomorrow; then, halfway home,
the return to check in case pipes would freeze.

Her giving is so easily absorbed. A thermostat
of concern smoothes the air. Earth mother. Fail-safe.
Heavy-footed angel I tread in with talk of
'staking out territory' and 'leaving it at that'.

Am I my mask? Our one-track compulsion to define
as a lavishness strives to expand our given space.
A sudden mantilla of doubt is shadowing her gaze:
'Why aren't we women as good at drawing the line?'

For a while, side by side, in the dusk we stood
and watched another shower, inhaling the slow
pervasion of a fall seizing on nothing, a mood
of persistence and letting be, its touch-and-go
decking spruces like brides, a mousse of zigzags
blurring and undoing the car's determined tracks.

La Différence

1 *Clash*

Suddenly you shrink – a carapace of pain.
Outsider I blunder further into protest.
Why? For heaven's sake try to explain.

Another wound. Hurt of a hurt unnoticed.
Can a man learn nothing but words? I bluster
clumsy half-sentences; thick-skinned, ham-fisted.

'If only you'd told me.' Instead you fester,
harbour a wordlessness that keeps trying to say
'to have to say is to fail'. My best filibuster

empties into silence. A mood leaves its highway
of huff-no-move stumbling towards self-reproach.
Am I the oafish male? And so we parley:

'If I were you I'd feel the same,' I approach
a sideways acknowledgement, a first breakthrough.
Words match words, the love-straws we clutch.

More the tomboy, more the sissy; atonement of two.
Dice of genes and *vive la différence.*
Woman me as I am manning you.

2 *Neighbour*

Me – possess you? See how I look
into your eye, human and similar.
I face a neighbour's face and talk
the common sense of common gender.

Much more the same than different:
fears, countless yearnings, our gauze
of meanings. So, by one consent
the welcome and appeal of face to face.

A delicate line of balance. But then
the rounds of your eyes grow murky,
the dark tips of your lashes lengthen,
a tremble in your aura caresses me.

Me – know you? So utterly more
different than the same. A modesty
absent in its presence, glory of desire;
something revealed, then drawn away.

3 *Nurses*

Staunch and calm in the dimmed light –
a charted pulse, a careful tuck –
I heed the dark sway of their bodies
as they keep watch, their rockabye
voices mothering towards sleep.

Where am I? Awareness sneaks
again to notice flushes of light,
lemon streaks of dawn re-establish
window-panes. I must have fallen off,
let ages slip through the sashes?

Allegro, full of good mornings
and how are we today Mr O'?
Girls with slender arms tidy
pillows, bring bowls of water
to swab and towel and daughter me.

Such young strides, such narrow waists!
They smile and know: born of women,
always theirs, they know beyond
my knowing. I yearn in their secret,
I sleep and wake in their wonder.

In the End

So I've confessed the cargo of my gender;
I know the subtle ways we've faced you down.
Maybe I've been more fortunate than others?

In the end I can only speak from experience.
I delight in womanhood. A marvel infinitely
refined. Nuances of strength. Their presence.

Together in everything, what veil of mystery
still falls between us? All I can't seize
seems to possess me. Comrade and mistress.

I love those tiny derailments of control
inviting me into the magnanimity of woman.
Unvisored. Somehow loosened in my role,

I wear a different mask, living and porous,
a delicious obedience to all my voices
allowing our musics their pitch and part.

Your freedom is our freedom. And I relearn
a forgotten register. Inward and airborne,
a soprano is gliding in my womanish heart.

Wisconsin

In May the Menomonie fishers show by the Lake
to spear some last treaty right in the shallows;
the local boys ride the water, jeer and smack
the waves, bucking their speedboat bronchos.

Someone, for God's sake, stop those bastards! Again
the absolute rage of youth: send back Mayflowers,
missioners with beads and guns, the frontiersmen,
caravels with their bellies full of conquistadores.

Our old indulgent dream of untouched races,
peace-pipe smokers, growers of squash and maize.
But they had drifted southward, married fur traders
and changed. Into the shifting muddle of what is

my anger blends. It's all too stitched in time,
the seams, the folds, the overlaps and patches.
Do you hear those outboard engines' scream?
We belong, we belong. Stop stabbing our conscience!

I think of Las Casas picking up the pieces
as regimes fall and one plan after another
sunders. He begins all over again; a business
unfinished, a ghost possessed by the word brother.

Doorway

I'd climbed the engineer's cabin steps, knocked
Like a schoolboy: Could I have a word with you?
There he stands in flannels, his navy blue
Blazer shining, framed by a door he's blocked.

'I'll give a man a hearing,' he says. I back
Downwards a little, still trying to glimpse
His face. It's London nineteen-sixty-six.
Whoever he thinks he sees is probably black

Or at best a step beneath. And I'm effaced.
I stand under sentence: guilt by motherland,
Overseen by some blindness I won't understand.
A degradation: such pride and so much waste.

But I grow older, begin to wonder if he
Like Plato's tyrant stared at empty space,
Confronting nothing and I was a shadow whose face
Had long turned away. I refuse this history.

I'm still climbing to a door, trying to retrace
Those steps. Tell me why you're afraid of me?
How lonely the eye in its majesty. See me.
Hold my gaze. I'm nothing but this naked face.

Shame

A mind already smitten;
rife and cloven cells,
alien vessels
of scorn doubling within.

In Pimlico Araners who shrank
when someone had spoken Irish,
a brand and blemish.
What would the Blacks think?

That African minister's rage;
his state-car blocked by a herdsman's
flock, he threatens
and shouts *Sauvage! Sauvage!*

Bitter moment of corrosion
when all that might have praised
turn to dust.
Iron eats into iron.

Progress

1

News of a truce broken. More shootings.
Young insurgents with sights fixed on square
one, some golden age about to rebegin.
A sweeping clean.
Always a flow in the flow of things,
will we ever start where we are?

Remember whose youth once fell for
loserdom, cragged faces of island people,
dream moment of a life standing still.
A glorious idol.
Or when it changed, how I'd begin to abhor
their cussedness, muddled and untameable.

Strange irony. Hairpin bend of fate.
The heart spawns our reason's overreach,
faces that moved us blur behind a veil
of pure ideal:
age-old lure of the clean slate,
of worlds begun from scratch.

2

The Suquamish kissing our earth as sister,
Antarchos the Greek centring the sun,
our Christ-Jew bannering the conquistador:
so much ravelled and then undone.

So many wisdoms won and suppressed
or the bitter foolishness of wisdom marred;
as if ground once gained is more than lost
and we keep returning in order to depart.

Something must love our rise, our lapses:
the contingent, the unforeseen, the fluent;
sideways and scrambled our tumbling process,
made or broken in the fullness of a moment.

Abel

I seem to follow the lure and flow of a story.
Then glimpses of a garden or a school dormitory
Shift and interchange. The frames begin to slip
Quicker than I understand. I'm losing my grip.
Why this crowd? And why are they hunting me?
Faster and faster. Suddenly I'm on a promontory,
The frenzy of chase closing its faceless threat.
Over the edge. I've woken in a snow of sweat.

Frenchie, let's get Frenchie. Again a tableau
Of schoolboy persecution sways in some undertow
Of memory. I hear the swishing wavelike noise
Of a mob in hot pursuit. Our ritual sacrifice.
A sallow and dapper stranger weaves and dodges
Down a corridor with a swarm of blurred visages
Close on his heels, whipping boy and scapegoat,
A swoon of oneness singling his difference out.

This evening in a country that I'd first come
To half a life ago, some blond youths loom
Up the platform, beer-cans glinting in the dark.
My suspicious swarthness. A Greek or even a Turk?
'Is it here we trounce foreigners?' sneers a voice,
Partly his show for the gang, partly his menace.
An ugly moment. I hurry on trying to pretend
I didn't understand, scanning exits for my friend.

Unbroken line of pogroms, this blindman's buff.
A planet now at stake, perhaps we know enough
To reveal even the slants and bias of our lens?
A stark figure transverses our shed millennia,
That first victim forever crying his innocence.
Stay the knife. Children of a jealous violence,
Fugitives on the earth, may we still ask his pardon?
Say to me, brother Abel, that I'm your guardian.

BOUNDARIES

Springbrunn är du, vars soligt glittrande stråle
skön i sin jämvikt, skön i sin formstränga båge,
skön i sin styrka, äger
makten att älska gränser och ädla mått.

A fountain you are, whose sunnily glittering beam,
beautiful in its equilibrium, beautiful in its form-strict arc,
beautiful in its strength, possesses
the power to love limits and noble dimensions.

KARIN BOYE
translated by David McDuff

Hopscotch

Our chalked figure of boxes squared
off and interlocked. Overlappings
of sides, t-shapes, half-shared
divides. A groundwork for high jinks.

'Your go!' And everyone hunkers to watch
if I toe the line. Footfall vigil.
Is this why the Germans call hopscotch
'playing a game of heaven and hell'?

Such passion for limits and thresholds.
Johnston's shop in Pettigo, its entrances
in both counties. A foot in two worlds.
Abutment and frontier. Old ambivalences.

Or the way sometimes exact same sounds
seemed to slide and play with words;
a child is riddling out how 'bounds'
means 'confines' and 'bounces forwards'.

Then, the pivot homewards. Our swift
about-face. Thrill and crisis of turning;
one ankle clasped, one hand aloft,
frail balance of gravity and yearning.

A skittish jump. Again our spreadeagle
heavy-footed landings astride a border.
Stop-go momentum of hop and straddle.
That need of lines. That leap's desire.

Noon

I've fallen in love again with gazing.
A lake is absorbing shimmered transfers
of grey alders and ripplings of leaves.

A hollow twig hesitates, then steers
outward, canoeing this ice-age maw.
Mountain eye. Basin of contemplation.

A skimmed stone tumbles and disappears.
Minutiae of an aeon. Noon is filling
the air with its riddles. Who am I?

Archaeologies of thought define me:
the words I use, phrases, gestures.
Is everything seen with an encoded eye?

Piecemeal layers of address and response.
Process of encounters: fall-out, settlings,
accruals, a womb of residues and ores.

Silent undertows. Still-living sediment.
A mountain lake swallows and endures
these slow, deep accumulations of sludge.

In the dark and light of every about-face
some beckoning aim, a hovering remembrance.
My spirit is watching over the waters.

Story

A man turns hostage for his friend's release:
It is a far, far better rest that I go to...
Abandon without return. Gratuity of sacrifice.

It is a far, far better thing that I do...
that cadenza of Dickens's *Tale of Two Cities*
and a child bursts in tears. Must it be so?

One story will haunt him all his living days.
The wartime girl with her German soldier flees
over the frontiers. Or tell him, now as he greys,

of an African spirit between one world and another
who stays around as a child just to make happy
the bruised face of a woman who'd become his mother.

My name is made illustrious in the light of his.
To break and enter another's brokenness and glory.

This is the story I'll touch in every caress.

Sunlight

Two children swimming out to the low tide rocks
and a woman watching. Breaststrokes. Headlong
aspirations of dips and bobs across the water.

Her lovely givenness a vigilance of substitution,
hostage to every breath and splash. Stange paradox:
the further they swim away, the nearer they are.

*'That's my place in the sun' is how the usurpation
of the whole world began.* And I fill with wonder
watching a woman watching. What is this reflex?

An abandon and weightlessness of concern. Pure
undergoing. Almost as if they float in the matrix
of her being, drifting in passivities of creation.

Some overflow of boundaries weaves its intrigues
of motherhood. A debt being payed before the loan,
as though she usurps herself in watching over

the whirl of their busy limbs oaring back water
in sunlight, the whole gown of her life turned
inside out. Her face glories in this reversal.

Some obsessive patience hears an ungiven order.
Does an echo somehow anticipate its sound?
She's so full of answers before they ever call.

Merging

Nursing your cold's fever I'm forever nine
Worrying by my mother's bedside years ago.

A blind is drawn low to guard her eyes from sunshine,
Slowly I wipe her brow with a sponge. It's as though

Two women are merging into one. I swab her hairline,
Breathing and undergoing all she'll have to undergo.

A sudden exhaustion seizes me. Now I watch for a sign.
Maybe she's begun to doze. I leave. Sneaking. Tiptoe.

I wanted to be the Samaritan pouring my oils and wine.
But was I some skulking Levite abandoning her pillow?

I know to serve you better I need to hold the line,
Yet where that line should go, how can I ever know?

Here nursing your fever will I be forever nine?
You gaze a gaze that seems to say: 'To think it's so,

To think for someone else even this face of mine
Is the face of a certain man going down to Jericho.'

Dusk

Look! a pair courting against the mauve
Of evening. Silhouettes caress on a bandstand,
Fold in their oneness. (Was it so long ago?)
We draw close and pass their no–man's-land
The first oblivion of kisses *quid pro quo*,
Those sweet trade-offs of *prima facie* love.

I glance their desire. Again a riddling elf
Of wisdom dances: are we only found in loss?
In going beyond our frontiers do we return?
Without reserve. Chosen even before I choose.
A first dalliance throws its nets of concern.
Matrices of care. Strange ecologies of self.

On a bench in fallen light that elderly couple
Tilt their bodies in a long mutual attention
Of nods and silence. Gestures seem to rehearse
Vigilant love-makings. Borders drawn or redrawn.
Drifts and siltings. All the brokerage of years.
A few strides apace and how far we travel.

Gull

An oilslick, jetsam of a tanker under
a flag of convenience and here's another
wing filmy and sealed, that waddle
of shame on the rocks a grounded gull
wide-eyed as a girl tarred and feathered.

Remember 'foe' and 'Erin' and 'liberty'?
The birds did whistle and sweetly sing
Changing their notes from tree to tree
The song they sang was old Ireland free.
Our innocence still a bird on the wing.

Who are we now? Our daily conspiracy
of mood and idioms, delta of memories,
names and quarrels of a shared place,
frail rootedness, complicities of ease,
womb of overlaps and shifting boundaries.

The rocks keep crumbling, trapping soil
in pioneer decays of lichen and moss;
some water-plant is netting in its root
the silt that clots a slobland. What
bird will nest its dream in our humus?

Sing the darker musics of complexity.

Image

Eighty miles or so from where I write
A divided house in love with an old hate
Feuds and kills. A ghostly tit for tat.
Bitter scores no one settles outright.

Even the terms are alien: 'Prod and Teague'.
Who are you neutral for and who against?
'Tar and featherings', 'kneecap punishments'.
Violence draws frontiers of a golden age.

World of black or white and perfect borders.
Verona or Belfast. It's brother on brother
In worlds long chequered into one another.
An X smeared on a wall. Evacuation orders.

Eighty miles I can't pretend to understand.
On screen tonight a woman mourns a childhood
Lover refound in middle age. Teague and Prod.
Eighty miles from here and still my island.

But I'm no Pilate. I can't now wash my hands,
For I too want these souring wounds to heal.
Those names! Drumshiel, Carn tSiadhail, Loch Shiel.
I'm mapped into landscapes of northern lands.

A woman's image is flying in the face of hate.
The lusts of eye for eye and blow for blow.
Somewhere let Capulet weep for fallen Romeo.
My Teague's hand reaches over a broken Juliet.

Parting

'I think of you often.' He nods
Knowingly. Parting he hugs me, pauses,
Then blurts 'alone in the woods
I've often seen
Your spirit darting among the spruces'.

I wanted to tell him before the train
Drew out how that morning I'd despaired
A wing rapped my window-pane,
A vehemence of friendship
Reaching out. And I wished I'd dared.

Radiance

Think of a black womb of nothingness.
An endless density. Then, it bursts.

A universe scatters through infinity.
The held momentum. The paced gravity.

As the helix tangles and grows complex,
Our feverish sun is a purse that leaks.

A knife-edge between chaos and leap.
Our running down and our building up.

At mutant rims, in my heart of confusion,
Some new and daring jumps of evolution.

Poem of becoming. Dance of detours.
Boundaries fall and a radiance endures.

The red giants die to zinc and carbon.
I grow with ashes of stars in my bone.

Music

Music, always music. And when the violins tumble
a thief has entered me.
Come and gone.
A sneaking anarchy
leaving spoors of memories I never had.

Incognito. Whimpers through crevices and pores,
quick bowings of a violin,
furious *pizzicato*
of what hasn't been
whinnies and hops beyond a future I imagine.

My vigilance breaks down. Rupture of being.
This syncopation. Offbeat,
out of phase
with myself, I vibrate.
What's this breathlessness I can't catch up with?

That flight of thirds mincing up a treble
clef. Lines of joy.
Matrix of frontiers.
EVERY GOOD BOY
DESERVES FAVOUR. Silences are spelling FACE.

Endless glory of some muteness that eludes me.
Approach of another face,
tremelo of forsakenness
naked and homeless.
How can I fold and suckle all its orphanhood?

Music, always music. Neighbour, are you the face
of that thief breaking in,
hollowing me out?
A tumbling violin
breathes its cries in me. I'm womb and mother.

Meditations

1 *After Niels Bohr*

Something in our nature enjoys twin truth.
An electron's double life: in turn a particle
And billow of guesses, waves of the probable.
Neither the one nor the other. World of both.

A thought in flows of the possible takes flesh.
Old Plato's lovely dream, undated and open;
The gain and shortfall of things as they happen.
Loves aims and journeys complement and mesh.

2 *After Alain Aspect*

Two quantums of light are shot contrariwise.
Then, pin one down travelling whatever line –
Already the other moves right-angled to its twin.
Separate togetherness. More a joy than surprise

As though the core knows what nothing has proved.
Unimaginable wholeness. A twitch in a filigree
Shimmers and ripples across a fragile city.
Of course, I still belong to anyone I've loved.

3 *After Werner Heisenberg*

Twin truths. And yet I can never gauge both.
Fix a particle and we've missed its impetus,
Fix its momentum and its place will elude us.
Every bid to fix catches us all in its truth.

Creation delights in this play of peekaboo.
I try to measure your nearness. You abscond.
Your gaze folds me into its infinite beyond.
Fugitive. Ungraspable. I can only love you.

The Bulldog O'Donnell

Chorus of tables and declensions. *Mensa, mensa.*
Latin or arithmetic. Both he'd made us sing
Aloud, his ruler slapping out a rhythm and pace.
Self-reliant and certain of gender and case.
'A sound mind in a sound body.' *Mens sana...*
Bulldog O'Donnell seemed so sure of everything.

Ah, the shattered self. How we'll fall to doubt.
Such tables turned, a temple tumbling down.
Our words. Our gender. Suspicion in commonplace.
Mistrust. Fragmentation. Irony's roundabout.
That long bony finger in the accusative case.
And who am I? All the whitened faces of a clown.

All my shed skins. But I hear him growing hoarse
With his questions: *What's the nominative in Latin?*
Who speaks? Who does what? Whose is the story?
Who's responsible for what? His own mandatory
Reply leading the choir: *The subject, of course!*
I ponder again the swish and metre of his baton.

My foibles, my moods, my myths. Even the sham.
For all that, I still weave a fragile city
Of trust. Blame me, friend. Praise me more.
What's best in me is what you love me for.
Our gazes intersect. And yes, here I am
So inconsistent, yet someone is counting on me.

Amo, amas, amat... He is pointing fingers
At himself, at me, at a neighbour. His chant
of boundaries: first, second and third person.
Conjugations of love. Was he really so certain?
That huge foot slamming the floor, a cincture's
Swayed scansion: *amamus, amatis, amant.*

FEAST

You must sit down, sayes Love, and taste my meat:
So I did sit and eat.

GEORGE HERBERT

Abundance

(for Marie)

To be there, childlike, when it happens.
Nothing I've ever earned or achieved.
Delight. Sudden quivers of abundance.

A whole glorious day with a friend.
Brunch. This honeyed bread. Talk.
All the time in the world to spend.

Those icy stings and a gladdened vein,
an autumn swim tingling my nape,
dousing pleasure on a sleepy brain.

Watching children on a bandstand floor;
some irrepressible urge to celebrate,
squealing, tramping, pleading for more.

November birches with leaves of apricot.
After a long walk in the frosty air,
to warm our palms around a coffee-pot.

Waves and moments of energy released.
I hoard them. A child with sweets and cakes
chortles at prospects of a midnight feast.

So much is that might never have been.

Pond

We'd been netting minnows in the pond all morning.
I knew he was palling with a boy from the avenue
I'd never liked. I still hear my jealous warning:
'If you play with him, then I won't play with you.'

Today a friend greeted me with a fleeting kiss,
Which seemed to glance traces of moments spun
To hours of lovemaking. Is it that I've known bliss?
That riddle of one in many, many in the one.

I remember how he'd smiled and didn't say a thing,
Just idly tossed a pebble to the middle of the pond.
Its plump and sucking fall expanded ring by ring.
A fiesta of hoops keeps swelling beyond and beyond.

Tight-Wire

Strolling fields behind the tent I glance
Figures leaving glares of light.
Wild applause inside.
Elephants to dance;
Now the acrobats delight
Children, now the juggling clown.
Someone hands a faded dressing gown.
Steadied, out she'll stride

Over guy-wires, over littered mud and cans
Past an empty pony stall
Slipping in among
Hung-out clothes and vans.
There she'll seem too small and frail.
No one saw who stepped the wire.
Those who clap her clap their own desire.
Someone always young

Slinging ropes between two garden sheds
Full of reckless festive grace
Seems to dare to flout
Endless overheads
Nothing underwrites but space.
Thrills of business just for fun
Touch the dreams of things we might have done.
Steadied, she'll step out.

Wireless

The word 'certain' and deep down I remember
a late-night newsreader's somnolent timbre
signing off just before the National Anthem.

A cabinet wireless square and solid as a world
around us, that row of knobs I'd once twirled
to eavesdrop on crackles and exotic noises

Riding the empty air. An innocence unravelled.
So much of what was certain a dominance veiled.
Suddenly it's a world multiple and bewildering

As foreign rumours and echoes we couldn't gag
when the tuning needle meandered over Europe:
Berlin, Stockholm, Paris, Hilversum, Prague.

Traces of static. An opulence breaking in.
I've grown to love the grit of interference.
Sizz and hubbub. So many cities of conversation.

Still a longing for the certain and overall.
To reach for timeless skies if only to fall
again into the deeper moments of what's ours.

Radio-waves vault to an overlayer and bounce.
A search for order in one man's resonance;
lives hueing and colouring the words we share.

Coherence hinted. A wager. Something guessed.
Echo of echo. Traces. Rumour of rumour.
This feast at which I'm both host and guest.

Michaelmas at Glendalough

Twin-lake valley scattered with remnants
Of praise and work and damp silence.
A path between the upper and lower lake
Greases with leaves. Is it the heartbreak
Of a season or the still ghosts of prayer
Hiding in birches? There's chill in the air,
Soon these leaves will fossilise in frost.
Something living stiffens and is lost.

Clusters of monks gathered in a first
Burgeoning, that strange lyrical outburst
Of separate worlds just newly spliced:
The lush blackbird, the eastern Christ.
I sense one watching from his beehive hut
As the upper lake gleams its sudden cross-cut
Of sunlight and epiphany and the lower lake
Clouds with all that's ordinary and opaque.

He stares. He'll bring his gleam of sun
To Europe after the Visigoth and Hun.
Will it all go so wrong? The dominance,
A loss of boundaries and shades of nuance.
Somehow everything's distant and mediated
The sacred blurs. Too veiled. Too weighted.
He's staring at an ideal. Let his face
Turn back to the shadows of the commonplace.

The lower lake darkens towards October.
He gazes. The waters are deep and sober.
Freedom and dignity, a love of the profane;
Some Luther is hallowing the ordinary again.
The best when spoilt will soon be worse:
Roundhead and votary of sweet commerce,
Then soiler and technocrat, a male caged
By a reason too controlled and disengaged.

Old ghosts of desire stir the undergrowth;
Two worlds and we crave the best of both
On this greasy path between two cisterns.
Michaelmas at Glendalough as a century turns.
My feastday. The air fills with fragility,
The choices and wounds of double polity.
Now in the shadows, now in the sun;
Can angels of this heart and mind be one?

Leisure

What does it mean?
Suddenly, effortlessly, to touch the core.
Mostly in the glow of friends
but today just strolling the length of a city street.
Carnival moments.
The apple back on its tree
in a garden lost, a garden longed for.

I move among traders.
Stacks of aubergines, rows of tiger-lilies.
Rings of silver and cornelian.
A feast of action.
Crosslegged, an Indian plays
music on a saw-blade glittering in the sun.

In the sweat of thy face
shalt thou eat bread. First hearing
that story, I'd bled for Adam.
I bump into an acquaintance and begin to apologise.
'Taking a break,
Be hard at it tomorrow'
Puritan me, so afraid of paradise.

Anaxagoras the sage
(a century before Plato) mulled it over
on a street like this in Athens.
First question: *Why are you here on earth?*
Answer: *To behold.*
No excuses called for.
Contemplation. Seeing. Fierce and intense.

This majesty. This fullness.
Does it all foreshadow another Eden?
The air is laden with yearning.
I can't say for what and I can't be silent either.
Rejoice. Rejoice.
To attest the gift of a day.
To saunter and gaze. To own the world.

Invitation

Anywhere and always just as you expect it least,
Welling or oozing from nowhere a desire to feast.

At Auschwitz Wolf hums Brahms' rhapsody by heart
As Eddy, thief turned juggler, rehearses his art.

Fling and abandon, gaieties colourful and porous.
The Mexican beggar's skirt, an Araner's *crios*.

Irresistable laughter, hiss and giggle of overflow.
That Black engine-driver crooning his life's motto:

'Paint or tell a story, sing or shovel coal,
You gotta get a glory or the job lacks soul.'

Abundance of joy bubbling some underground jazz.
A voice whispers: Be with me tonight in paradise.

Celebration

Once our days were years. Now years are days.
A guest glances a clock on a kitchen shelf
As though he'd suddenly woken from a daze:
It's gone so fast I must have enjoyed myself.

The tiniest ticks in glacial ages of stones
Or even less on crueller scales of stars;
A man with dreams of past and future zones
Loses a self in aeons of clocks and calendars.

Lines with loops of days or months or years.
We don't know how to begin to think of time:
Memory, expectation, our shy hopes and fears –
Easier to word the taste of mango with lime.

Which Native American people used to say:
We never come to time, it comes to us?
Unwind the clock and let it come as it may,
Turn or spiral, a plot thickening and viscous.

But image on image seems to return to one:
A medium in which our doings move, a continuity
Inscribed and cummulative, all done or undone
A chain of traces across a fragile city.

Delicate filigree. Tables of face-to-faceness,
Years of talk and laughter's shooting star.
The healing moment mango and lime caress.
To choose to say we're glad we've come so far.

Expectation

Waiting for you it's all those years ago,
Flutters of courtship smile in your approach.
Is it the gypsy earrings, the enamelled broach,
Native amber beads I'd brought from Chicago?

Doublespeak of dress that hides and flirts.
Little hoists of ceremony: tilts of a cap,
Hints of calves fattening over an ankle strap.
A giddiness of feasting gathers in dusky skirts.

Delight

Let the meal be simple. A big plate
of mussels, warm bread with garlic,
and enough mulled wine to celebrate

Being here. I open a hinged mussel
pincering a balloon of plump meat
from the blue angel wings of a shell.

A table's rising decibels of fun.
Such gossip. A story caps a story.
Banter. Then, another pun on a pun.

Iced yoghurt snipes at my temples.
My tongue matches a strawberry's heart
with its rough skin of goose-pimples.

Conversations fragment. Tête-à-tête,
a confidence passes between two guests.
A munch of oatcake thickens my palate.

Juicy fumes of a mango on my breath.
(A poem with no end but delight.)
I knife to the oblong host of its pith.

Wine sinks its ease to the nerve-ends.
Here are my roots. I feast on faces.
Boundless laughter. A radiance of friends.

Courtesy

1

I bring my basketful to serve
Our table. Everything mine is yours.
Everything. Without reserve.

Poems to which I still revert.
Gauguin. Matisse. Renoir's pear-shaped women.
Music I've heard. Blessed Schubert.

Ecstasies I'll never understand –
Mandelstam's instants of splendour, the world
A plain apple in his hand.

Lost faces. Those whose heirs
I was. My print-out of their genes,
Seed and breed of forbears.

Whatever I've become – courtesy
Of lovers, friends or friends of friends.
All those traces in me.

The living and dead. My sum
Of being. A host open and woundable.
Here I am!

2

Tiny as a firefly under the night sky,
We try to imagine stars that travel
Two million light years to reach the eye.

Long ago on a stormy and starless night
Old people used keep a half-door opened,
Anyone passing could make for the light.

The Russian astronauts leaving after them
Bread and salt for the next to dock
At the station. Small symbols of welcome.

Who's that outsider waiting for you?
We try to imagine how destinies unravel
Across the years towards their rendezvous.

A space for wanderers, lone or dispossessed.
At this table we've laid one empty place,
That old courtesy for the missing guest.

3

Never again just this.
Once-off. Ongoing wistfulness.
Wine loosening through my thighs.
Closeness. Our sudden huddle of intimacy.
These hours we're citizens of paradise.

A nourishment of senses.
Such fierce delight tenses
Between affections and the moments
When, like a theatre after its applause,
This house will fall again to silence.

Let gaieties outweigh
Their own misgivings. Emigré
And native, my desire attends
The moment in and out of time
Which even when it ceases never ends.

I feed on such courtesy.
These guests keep countenancing me.
Mine always mine. This complicity
Of faces, companions, breadbreakers.
You and you and you. My fragile city.

Dance

1 *Weaving*

So tables aside! Any dance at all.
I'd loved our flight from the formal.
Our broken observance. Rock and Roll.
The Twist. Disco. Sweet and manic,
Our blare of rapture. Alone. Freelance.
But I yearn again for ritual, organic
Patterns, circlings, the whorled dance.

Sweated repetitiveness of reels that grew
To their ecstasy. A shrug. Yelped *yeoo*.
Quadrilles without the high buckled shoe,
Ribboned wigs, swallow-tailed elegance
Of Napoleon's court or Paris ballroom,
Figures needling an embroidery of dance,
Chaine-de-dames. Fan and perfume.

More a passionate sameness than grace.
Hospitality. Feelings of inclusiveness
As we lined up there. Face to face.
Expectant. Keats's lovers in the gaze
Of a moment but ready to step it out
Across the swollen belly of a vase.
Tableaux of memory wake in that shout:

Take the floor! The first battoned tone
Of a *céilí* band. *The Mason's Apron*,
Humours of Bandon. *The Bridge of Athlone*.
A swing. A turn. The skipping march.
Limerick's Walls, *The Siege of Ennis*.
Side-step and stoop under the arch.
Our linked arms. A scent of dizziness.

Openness. Again and again to realign.
Another face and the moves must begin
Anew. And we unfold into our design.
I want to dance for ever. A veil
Shakes between now-ness and infinity.
Touch of hands. Communal and frail.
Our courtesies weave a fragile city.

2 *Play*

Is music a love-making? To dance in rhythm,
our bodies sharing these humours and fancies.

Low-necks. Just glimmers of beautiful limbs.
The changing and same ballet of intimacies.

Yet all that talk of 'playing with fire'.
The puritans have put us through our paces.

Dante's lustful shades were doing time
relearning for eternity swift embraces.

This arm around my waist. That shoulder
leaning on mine the freight of its histories.

Blouses. Men with cummerbunds. The gleam
and sizzle of dresses. To glorify what is.

No matter what this dance will be here.
Blessed be its weavings and its intricacies.

O fragile city of my trust and desire!
Our glancings. No longer any need to possess.

Tiny dalliances. Middle ground of playfulness.
This dance shuffling our warmth as we pass.

3 *Glimpse*

A few are sitting this one out: spectators,
Thinkers on the outside, catching a glance
Of how the dancers turn like Plato's stars.

Dance in a cosmos, cosmos in the light of dance.
An ancient image, I know, stuff of visionaries:
Harmony, music of spheres, the mystic's trance.

The whirl of it! Barefaced and fluid boundaries,
I'm watching through a window, sipping iced beer
In the night air. Ripe images. Old quandaries.

To dance between infinites of quark and star,
Lost in a labyrinth we ourselves have planned.
Detached and involved. Half-god, half-creature.

Glimpse from a stillness beyond rhythm's command.
An inner stillness in the shifting views of dancers.
To stand under heavens you can never understand.

Rhythm of now. Now the beat.
Forever. Forever.
Our *qui vive* of listening feet.
Sweetest seizure.

Such ecstasies as maddened Corybants:
A *bodhrán*'s crescendo,
Frenzy of bones knuckling the dance,
High wire of let-go.

A reel with all its plans. Drumbeat,
Steps or turns,
Stubborn ritual. Some dizzy heat
Of spirit yearns.

Forever. Forever. How to remember
In each move and pose,
Even the music's pitch and timbre
Crave repose?

Leaps in an infinite womb. I yield.
The dance's yes
Teeters on the rim of Achilles' shield.
Vertigo of gladness.